i follow

Connecting Belief and Behavior
to Who You Are in Christ

SCOTT SIMMONS

wesleyan
publishing
house

Indianapolis, Indiana

ifollow

Copyright © 2009 by Wesleyan Publishing House
Published by Wesleyan Publishing House
Indianapolis, Indiana 46250
Printed in the United States of America
ISBN: 978-0-89827-399-1

Cover design by Kory Pence.

CONTENTS

CRASH

{ For I know the plans I have for you . . . plans to prosper you and not to harm you, plans to give you hope and a future. }

—Jeremiah 29:11

A group of rhinoceroses is called a *crash*.

It seems kind of strange at first until we understand the reasoning. Rhinos can run thirty miles per hour but can only see thirty feet in front of them.

Crash is a good word for what happens to us when we run with no purpose or vision in our lives. However, you were created with a purpose in mind, and when you begin to understand God's plans, you will be able to run with full force into a life of fulfillment and purpose.

This year in the United States alone:

- 74.5 million students will be enrolled in kindergarten through twelfth grade.

- 9.9 million, or nearly 20 percent of those school-age kids, speak a language other than English at home.

- 2.9 million high school diplomas will be awarded at the end of the school year.

It is easy to get lost in this world. But God did not create you to get lost in the shuffle of life. He has a plan for your life. You were created for a reason that can only be found in Christ Jesus. John 10:10 tells us that Jesus came so that we would have an abundant life. *iFollow* is created to help you trust in Jesus and discover the ultimate plan for your life.

HOW THE BOOK WORKS

iFollow contains ten lessons. Each lesson has five sections:

1. Getting Started—prepares your mind and heart to listen to God's Word.

2. Discovering the Truth—presents God's Word as a guide to life.

3. Embracing the Truth—explains the Word of God and how it addresses real life.

4. Connecting the Truth—relates the Word of God to your life.

5. Bringing It Home—reflects on how God's Word should show up in your everyday life.

Many students will work through this book with a mature Christian who can serve as a mentor for discipleship. The next section of this book provides guidance for those serving as discipleship mentors.

Finishing a ten-week discipleship series does not necessarily make you a disciple. But it can put you on a path to gaining understanding of God's plan for your life while developing disciplines that strengthen you for the journey. Discipleship is measured by growth, so go and grow in Christ.

A WORD TO DISCIPLESHIP MENTORS

Spiritual formation—becoming what God has created you to be—is the main theme of this book. It's also the theme for the entire history of our church—The Wesleyan Church. With great pride in God's work in our history and current lives, we are confident in our stance that all of us can surrender our lives completely to God and live a pure life in our words, thoughts, and actions every day.

To be a disciple of God means we're serious about living totally committed, pure lives for God in a world that wants to shut him up and out. He's promised to help us succeed in living to please him. With his help, it's possible to live a life that is not addicted to or trapped by sin. While sin is all around us, the Holy Spirit of God is available at all times to help us all say no to sin and yes to right living.

True followers of Christ are interested in becoming more and more like him. Knowing how to follow Jesus is easy, but actually following Jesus day in and day out remains the challenge. The truth is that there is great worth found in the journey of following after Jesus Christ.

The goal of *iFollow* is to connect every teen to a solid relationship with Jesus. The scope of what teens can do for Jesus is limitless. *iFollow* helps students embrace the challenge of walking with Christ daily and puts students on the right path to find significance, value, and impact as Christians.

iFollow comes with a built-in expectation that those walking with Christ will actually live out what they are studying. It's not enough to fill our heads and hearts with Jesus. We must follow through, making sure his love for and interest in others shows up in our service and daily activities. In other words, walking with Christ is best done when we use our entire being: head, heart, hands, and habits.

As a youth leader, worker, or pastor, you have an awesome privilege and responsibility to care for and mentor students in your realm of influence. *iFollow* is a resource that both you and your students can use to shape their lives into the image of God.

This book is not a substitute for your active involvement in your students' lives. Instead, use this book as a guide for developing and discipling your students. Give your students a copy and then meet with each student once a week to discuss the week's lesson, encourage their walk, and hold them accountable in pursuing after Christ.

May God bless you richly as you invest in the lives of the students he has given into your care!

IMAGE

It is easy to fall into the trap of looking around and comparing yourself to others. Am I as skinny as her? Is my car as sweet as his? Am I doing better in school? Am I more popular? It can even happen with the things of God: Do I pray more or read my Bible more than them? Following Jesus is not about how you stack up against others; it is about loving God and loving others—and this looks like being who God created you to be.

IMAGE

It's disturbing to think that your entire existence as a human being might be measured by these few things:

- Your name: Whom do you belong to? Where do you come from?

- What you do: What's your profession? How much money do you make?

- How you look: Do you have style? Are you attractive?

As a society, we hang our hats on these things, as if where you're from and what you do provides a snapshot of the real you.

What would you say if someone asked you to share your story? Seriously. What would you say?

How you see yourself has a lot to do with how others see you. Your image is everything on the inside that you choose to project outward. And it comes out in all forms. Your style, the way you express yourself, physical fitness, personal appearance, and even how you spend your money are great measuring sticks of the stuff going on inside you.

Just stop for a minute and ask yourself this question: How does God see me? You may be surprised by the answer. Knowing who you are in Christ and how God sees you will provide solid ground to walk on as you begin the journey of following Christ.

GETTING STARTED

What's Your Style?

Answer these questions to begin thinking about your personal style.

1. It's Saturday morning and your mom wants you to run to the grocery store for milk and flour. Do you:

   a. throw on a hat and sweats, forget the rest, grab the keys, and go?

   b. brush your hair and teeth, wash your face, grab the keys, and go?

   c. take an hour or so to shower, clean up, pick out an outfit, grab the keys, and go?

2. You have a hole in the sole of your shoes. Do you:

    a. get some duct tape and work some magic?

    b. buy whatever is affordable, choosing comfort over fashion?

    c. bug your folks to death until they buy you a new pair?

3. Paris Hilton just crashed your best friends' party and you:

    a. wonder who the new girl is.

    b. think it's totally inappropriate for anyone to crash a party.

    c. wonder where she gets her clothes and if she can hook you up with some connections.

When it comes to thinking about how you see yourself and how others see you, you have to find a healthy balance. Not caring at all about your image can be as bad as spending too much time concerned about image. You are an original, one of a kind person, so be true to yourself and find your confidence in Christ.

DISCOVERING THE TRUTH

{ Our subconscious minds have no sense of humor, play no jokes, and cannot tell the difference between reality and an imagined thought or image. What we continually think about eventually will manifest in our lives. }

—Robert Collier

When God sees you, what does he think about you? When he sees you stripped of all the images you put up—vulnerable, standing fully exposed in the light of his brilliance, unable to hide anything—what do you suppose he thinks about you?

Read the following verses to gain some insight. Write the value God places on your life based on how he sees you. The first one is done for you.

Scripture	Truth	Value
Genesis 1:26–27	I am created in the image of God.	I have self-worth.
Psalm 139:13–16		
John 3:16		
Ephesians 2:10		
Matthew 9:36		

Before the fall of humanity (Adam and Eve's sin in the Garden of Eden), God and his people lived in perfect relationship with one another. Then sin entered the scene and drove a wedge between us and the Creator. Think about this: God puts a lot of value on your life. So much so that he sent his Son to die for your sins as a way to bridge the gap sin created.

EMBRACING THE TRUTH

You take on a whole new identity when you receive Christ as Savior. According to 2 Corinthians 5:21, if you have received Christ you now have the righteousness of God on you. That should change the way you view yourself. Everything you do from this point on should be rooted in that fact.

On the chart below, list the various characteristics that describe what Christ is like and what you are like.

Christ-likeness	Me-likeness
_____	_____
_____	_____
_____	_____
_____	_____
_____	_____
_____	_____

Look again at the chart. Note the differences. Are there any similarities? If Christ is living in you, all the factors on the left should be evidenced in your life in one way or another.

CONNECTING THE TRUTH

Relax. Realize that your walk with Christ is one that begins right where you are and transforms you into the person God created you to be. Read the following verses and be encouraged.

"Therefore, if anyone is in Christ, he is a new creation; the old has gone, the new has come!" (2 Corinthians 5:17).

"But you are a chosen people, a royal priesthood, a holy nation, a people belonging to God, that you may declare the praises of him who called you out of darkness into his wonderful light" (1 Peter 2:9).

"How great is the love the Father has lavished on us, that we should be called children of God! And that is what we are! The reason the world does not know us is that it did not know him" (1 John 3:1).

"Jesus said to the people who believed in him, 'You are truly my disciples if you remain faithful to my teachings'" (John 8:31 NLT).

BRINGING IT HOME

[At Rex Kwan Do, we use the buddy system. No more flying solo. You need somebody watching your back at all times. Second off, you're gonna learn to discipline your image. You think I got where I am today because I dressed like Peter Pan over here?]

—Rex from *Napoleon Dynamite*

Rejoice in the fact that you have this new self that's being renewed in knowledge in the image of its Creator. Who you are is now defined by who you are in Christ and not by what this world says you need to be. According to Philippians 4:13, what needs to take place to begin such a transformed life?

_____

_____

_____

You're not alone, and it's not up to just you. Christ in you gives you strength, identity, and purpose.

Webster defines *identity* as "the name or essential character that identifies somebody or something." What or who is the essential character that identifies you?

_____

_____

_____

Remember that everything we put stock into in this world will fade away. Jesus assures us that he will never leave us nor forsake us. That promise should bring confidence to your life.

Read Romans 12:1–2 and list the three main things we as believers are instructed to do as we discover our new identity in Christ.

1. _____

2. _____

3. _____

FOLLOW

The call to follow Jesus is radically countercultural. But what is it that really sets Christians apart from the world? What could possibly motivate us to say "No" to our sinful desires when the world is saying "Go for it"? It boils down to a relationship with the living God. To follow is a choice to trust his love and plan for your life.

FOLLOW

Some people think students have a problem committing. In reality, all kinds of people are committed to following all kinds of things: hobbies, YouTube, Facebook, sports, music, Bible reading, skateboarding, pizza, sleeping in, Dippin' Dots, tanning booths, NASCAR. You name it, people are committed to it. They spend loads of time chasing after things, a lot of which could be considered nonsense.

When it comes to your commitments about what or who you follow, ask this question: Will this last, or is it going to fade away someday?

Why not commit your time, energy, and direction toward something that will be around forever? Think about things you could do today and this week that will last for eternity.

GETTING STARTED

Rate the influence of the following historical and current leaders on a scale from 1 to 10, with 1 being the least influence and 10 the greatest influence.

Winston Churchill	1	2	3	4	5	6	7	8	9	10
Martin Luther King, Jr.	1	2	3	4	5	6	7	8	9	10
Abraham Lincoln	1	2	3	4	5	6	7	8	9	10
Bill Clinton	1	2	3	4	5	6	7	8	9	10
Julius Caesar	1	2	3	4	5	6	7	8	9	10
Franklin D. Roosevelt	1	2	3	4	5	6	7	8	9	10
Gandhi	1	2	3	4	5	6	7	8	9	10
Adolf Hitler	1	2	3	4	5	6	7	8	9	10
Barack Obama	1	2	3	4	5	6	7	8	9	10
Billy Graham	1	2	3	4	5	6	7	8	9	10

Why do you think people are (or were) so inclined to follow these individuals?

_____

_____

_____

What are (or were) some of their primary characteristics?

_____

_____

_____

What do you look for in a leader?

_____

_____

_____

Whom or what do you follow?

_____

_____

_____

DISCOVERING THE TRUTH

{ Following the light of the sun, we left the Old World. }
—Christopher Columbus

In order for one to follow, one must know whom to follow. In this world we hear many voices screaming at us to follow them. The bottom line is that all of our lives we follow someone—parents from birth to adulthood; teachers in school who develop our minds; popular trends and fashion as we seek to fit in and find acceptance; sports and academics all lead us down one path or another. Who you are *today* is based on whom or what you decided to follow *yesterday*. Who you will become *tomorrow* will always be based on whom or what you follow today.

Read the following verses:

- Colossians 3:10

- 2 Corinthians 5:17

- Ephesians 4:21–24

Based on the verses above, what is God's goal for the Christian?

_____

_____

_____

What is the ultimate aim?

_____

_____

_____

Our new life in Christ brings new paths and directions. We may have to stop following some people or things to receive God's blessings. However, it is not enough to stop following one lifestyle; we have to start following another.

EMBRACING THE TRUTH

What are some excuses people use for not following Jesus?

_____

_____

_____

What are some false concepts of who Jesus is?

_____

_____

_____

If you are going to follow Jesus, you should know who he truly is. Read the following verses to identify who Jesus is:

- Hebrews 4:15 _____

- Hebrews 7:26 _____

- John 3:2 _____

- John 14:6 _____

Why should you choose to follow Jesus?

_____

_____

_____

The influence Jesus had on the lives of people has never been surpassed. No other great leader has inspired so many positive changes in the lives of his or her followers. People who encounter the risen Christ are totally transformed. Their outlook on life is altered forever. Staying true to their faith, they do not hesitate to face hardship, persecution, and even death. Many have found fulfillment and joy in following the teachings of Jesus. Your life was transformed when you met Christ and yielded yourself to him.

CONNECTING THE TRUTH

Here is a list of verses that give different names and attributes of Christ. Look at each verse and determine how your life can be transformed by following and trusting in Jesus. The first one is done for you as an example.

Text	Name	Application
Revelation 22:13	Alpha and Omega	He is eternal; I can trust him forever.
Isaiah 9:6	_____	_____
Hebrews 1:2	_____	_____
Matthew 1:23	_____	_____
Mark 6:3	_____	_____
1 Timothy 2:5–6	_____	_____
John 8:12	_____	_____
John 15:1–2	_____	_____

BRINGING IT HOME

Jesus tapped me on the shoulder and said,
"Bob, why are you resisting me?"

I said, "I'm not resisting you!"

He said, "You gonna follow me?"

I said, "I've never thought about that before!"

He said, "When you're not following me,
you're resisting me."

—Bob Dylan

When you read Philippians 2:5–11, what about Jesus' life appeals to you?

_____

_____

_____

It can never be said that Christ requires of his followers what he did not demonstrate himself.

Where's the starting point in your life in order for you to follow Jesus?

_____

_____

_____

What are some things you must let go of to move forward?

_____

_____

_____

In John 14:21, Jesus promises to reveal himself and his love to those who love and obey him. In what ways do you need to be obedient in your new walk with Christ?

_____

_____

_____

LOVE

When you're hungry, you crave food, right? When you're lonely, you crave company, right? Have you ever had a craving to make a difference with your life? These are healthy cravings. But what about when you're jealous, and you crave something that is not yours? How about the cravings of lust, revenge, or greed? How can we tell the difference between healthy cravings and the "cravings of sinful man"? *Love.*

LOVE

It's amazing the things we do in the name of love. Who you are and what you do is a result of whom or what you love. Love is what sustains the walk. Love fuels the passion for the journey of following Jesus Christ. As you grow in your love for God, you will walk as Jesus walked. It was the power of love that took Jesus to the cross. It was for love that God sent his Son in the first place.

When you look at the character and attributes of God, you can't help but develop a deep love for the Creator. Receiving the great love of God should move us to a place where we show love to others. In fact, Jesus tells those who follow him that people will know you by your love. A great witness to our walk is when we show love for others. This isn't the mushy, sappy kind of love, but the kind found in John 15:12, where Jesus commands us to "Love each other as I have loved you."

GETTING STARTED

[I'm not a smart man . . . but I know what love is.]

—Forrest Gump

Read the following scenarios and mark which category best describes your feelings:

Going to the movies

    love it   *like it*   *leave it*

High School Musical

    love it   *like it*   *leave it*

Facebook

    love it   *like it*   *leave it*

Chinese arithmetic

    love it   *like it*   *leave it*

Shopping

    love it   *like it*   *leave it*

Text messaging

    love it   *like it*   *leave it*

High school football

    love it   *like it*   *leave it*

DISCOVERING THE TRUTH

 The hunger for love is much more difficult to remove than the hunger for bread.

—Mother Teresa

Life is full of emotions. We like things, love things, and sometimes even hate things. Jesus tells us in his Word to "'Love the Lord your God with all your heart and with all your soul and with all your strength and with all your mind'; and, 'Love your neighbor as yourself'" (Luke 10:27). The interesting thing about this verse is that loving is a command. When Jesus tells us to love God, he's not making a suggestion; it's a command.

We often think we *cannot* love something or someone when the truth is that love is a choice. We all have the ability to choose whom or what we love. Understanding the character and nature of God will help you see the love he has for us and will give you reason to love him in return. Look at the following Scriptures and write how God chose to love us and the value it brings to our life.

Scripture	Act of Love	Value
Psalm 27:1		
Jeremiah 9:23		
John 3:16		
Romans 8:37–39		
2 Corinthians 4:7–9		

It doesn't take long to begin to see God's love for us and all that it brings to our lives. The key to growing and walking in the Lord is to understand this love. There's nothing we can do to earn God's love. To strive to be holy or to achieve our mission in life in order to earn more of Christ's love is wrong motivation. Jesus loves us. Period. He doesn't love us based on what we do, but for who we are.

EMBRACING THE TRUTH

[
Love so amazing, so divine,
Demands my soul, my life, my all.
—"When I Survey the Wondrous Cross"
]

Now that you have an understanding of God's love for us, take a look at what God says about love. Read 1 Corinthians 13:4–7, and start naming what God says love is.

_____
_____
_____
_____
_____
_____

God's view on love doesn't always match the world's view on love. Take a look at the list above and compare it to the world's view. You've read what God says about love. List the differences on the next page.

God says	World says
Love is patient.	_____
Love does not envy.	_____
Love does not boast.	_____
Love is not rude.	_____
Love keeps no record of wrongdoing.	_____
Love always perseveres.	_____
Love never fails.	_____

CONNECTING THE TRUTH

{ The Lord will fulfill his purpose for me; your love, O Lord, endures forever—do not abandon the works of your hands. }

—Psalm 138:8

God's love compels us. It motivates us. David the psalmist knew this when, in a high state of emotion on the day he was finally rescued from his relentless enemies, he wrote in simple, plain, down-to-earth words: "I love you, LORD" (Psalm 18:1 NLT). Not stopping there, David then felt compelled to explain his feelings by proclaiming, "The LORD is my rock, my fortress, and my savior; my God is my rock, in whom I find protection. He is my shield, the power that saves me, and my place of safety" (Psalm 18:2 NLT).

Proclaiming and receiving the love of the Lord elevates your life. It lifts the downcast soul and makes the godly "flourish like palm trees" (Psalm 92:12 NLT). This love also comes from an expression of a satisfied soul. The love of God and for God moves the soul to cry out, "You thrill me, LORD, with all you have done for me!" (Psalm 92:4 NLT). The love of God elevates our life.

BRINGING IT HOME

Earlier you listed all the things God said about love in 1 Corinthians 13. Go back and look at your list and answer the following questions:

Which do you have a hard time saying honestly?

_____

_____

_____

Which statement or quality would you say you need to work on most?

_____

_____

_____

Make it a matter of prayer and begin to look for opportunities to put that love into practice. These things may not be easy to master. But you have the Holy Spirit inside of you to encourage and help you along the way. Remember that when you express any of these qualities, you're expressing your love toward God. With that kind of love in your heart, you will in turn love others more naturally, because God will love others through you.

PRAY

You can't have a lasting relationship with God without talking to him, just as relationships with friends won't last, if you don't talk to them. You may wonder if you are praying the "right" way. God hears and understands the intention of your heart. There is no "right" or "wrong" way to pray. As you communicate with God on a consistent basis, your life will begin to be full, as your relationship with Jesus grows.

PRAY

How do you know if you really know God? What enables you to believe in an unseen God so much that he moves your life as you surrender to him? John Woodruff represented the United States in the 800 meters at the 1936 Olympics in Berlin. In the middle of the race, feeling crowded by the pack, he stopped and let everyone pass him. Then, running on the outside, he passed them all to win the gold medal.

It's in those moments when we stop that we get to know God and then are able to move forward more freely and effectively. How well do you know God and the direction he is giving you for your life? Make it a practice to stop regularly and commune with God. By doing so, you will actually move along faster.

GETTING STARTED

Name someone you know well enough (not someone you know about, such as Abraham Lincoln, but someone you know personally) to give details about his or her life. Write the name here.

_____

How do you know that person? Think beyond just "parent" or "friend." How do you really know that person? List six reasons that make you confident you really know this person.

1. _____

2. _____

3. _____

4. _____

5. _____

6. _____

DISCOVERING THE TRUTH

Read the following Scripture verses and list the ways God communicates with us.

Hebrews 1:1 _____

Matthew 2:12 _____

Matthew 28:5 _____

Luke 3:22 _____

Exodus 31:18 _____

Romans 16:26 _____

Judges 6:38 _____

Ephesians 6:1–2 _____

Proverbs 11:14 _____

Hebrews 1:2 _____

Just as we grow closer to our parents, boyfriend, girlfriend, and friends by spending time and talking with them, the same principle is true when it comes to growing closer to God. Prayer (communication with God) is crucial in following God and the journey he has for you. Time and time again we see God in constant communication with us. It's no wonder that we are a relational people, because God is a relational God. And if we are created in God's image (and we are!), then it only stands to reason that we have the internal desire to have community and meaningful relationships. God speaks to you. Are you listening?

EMBRACING THE TRUTH

Do not be anxious about anything, but in everything,
by prayer and petition, with thanksgiving,
present your requests to God.

—Philippians 4:6

Paul tells us in the Word to seek God and bring requests, concerns, worries, and praise to him. Just as God wants to communicate with us, he desires for us to communicate with him. In Jesus, we can see an accurate example of a person who knows the power and effectiveness of prayer. Measure the pattern of Jesus' prayer life on the following scale:

He prayed frequently.

| solid | 1 | 2 | 3 | 4 | 5 | 6 | 7 | weak |

He prayed with conviction.

| solid | 1 | 2 | 3 | 4 | 5 | 6 | 7 | weak |

He prayed in making decisions.

| solid | 1 | 2 | 3 | 4 | 5 | 6 | 7 | weak |

He prayed for long periods of time.

| solid | 1 | 2 | 3 | 4 | 5 | 6 | 7 | weak |

He prayed by himself.

| solid | 1 | 2 | 3 | 4 | 5 | 6 | 7 | weak |

He prayed with others.

| solid | 1 | 2 | 3 | 4 | 5 | 6 | 7 | weak |

According to Hebrews 7:25, what is Jesus doing right now?

_____

_____

_____

CONNECTING THE TRUTH

[
To be a Christian without prayer is no more possible
than to be alive without breathing.

—Martin Luther King, Jr.
]

Did you know that the only recorded reference of the disciples asking Jesus to teach them something was when they wanted to learn how to pray? Think about it. They could have asked Jesus to teach them any number of things—how to walk on water, heal the sick, perform miracles, or reveal mysteries of the Old Testament. However, in Luke 11:1, we find the only request recorded by the disciples as being "teach us to pray."

Jesus gives us a perfect model of prayer in Matthew 6:9–13, as well as Luke 11:2–4. Take a look at the prayer, dissect it, and embrace the power within the words.

The Prayer	The Meaning	The Application
Our Father	Acknowledges who God is	Understand the relationship
Hallowed be	God is holy	Give praise and adoration
Your kingdom	God's will over yours	Express desire to know God
Daily bread	God's provision	Show thankfulness, gratitude
Forgive us	God's mercy	Ask for forgiveness
Lead us	God's protection	Seek refuge, find safety
Deliver us	God's guidance	Freedom found in God

There are all kinds of reasons to pray. Some people pray when they're scared, when they're in great need, or when there seems no other way. So, how about it? When and why do you pray?

In Luke 18, Jesus tells his disciples to always pray and never give up. Think about it. He is talking to his disciples, those who were committed to him. If you're truly committed to following Jesus, then you should be a person of prayer. It's the open door to getting to know God in an intimate way. Take a look at the Word and the many reasons why you should be committed to prayer.

Scripture	Why pray
Philippians 4:6–7	to receive peace
Matthew 7:7–8	to receive God's blessings
John 16:24	to receive joy
James 1:5	to receive wisdom
James 4:8	to come close to God
Matthew 26:41	to not fall into temptation
Psalm 91:15	to be protected

BRINGING IT HOME

It's boring

I don't know what to say.

I forget.

I usually fall asleep.

It seems like I never have time.

I can't stay focused.

God never answers my prayers.

These excuses sound familiar? Or maybe you don't really understand prayer. Maybe you've been going about it the wrong way. You may feel you don't know how to pray or you're not sure what to expect from your prayers. Here's the deal:

- If you're praying that God would make you famous, you're praying the wrong way.

- If you pray that God would make the answers to the test you didn't study for appear in your mind, you're not getting it.

- If you're praying that you would win the lottery, have superpowers, or for the protection of your favorite TV character, then you really need to step back and grab hold of your life.

If your prayer life is full of excuses, confess to God and admit there really is no excuse. Ask God to help you to seek the true value in prayer. It can be powerful and productive. Then remember the steps to genuine prayer.

Pray with Conviction

We must believe God is not only capable, but also willing to meet our request. Pray believing in an all-powerful God. Have the confidence that your words carry weight with God. He cares about you. Believe that he has the best in store for you.

Pray in Line with God's Word

It's useless to pray for something outside of God's Word. Answered prayer is always in sync with Scripture. The more you know God's Word, the more effective your prayers will become. Read and learn from the prayers found in the Bible. Jesus' prayer in John 17 and David's prayers in Psalms give you great words and attitudes you can use in your own conversation with God.

Be Specific

Don't just pray for God's healing. List it out: "Help my dad find a job" or "Deliver my mother from cancer." If you're not specific in your request, how will you know when the prayer is answered?

Trust God enough to stop generalizing, and open up and share from your heart. You will find that specific prayers will get specific answers.

Pray Expecting Answers

Anticipate that God will answer. Claim Matthew 7:7—"Ask and it will be given to you; seek and you will find; knock and the door will be opened to you." Know that you're not just shooting up a request in hopes that God will hear it. God cares and he will answer. When you pray, pray as Jesus prayed—that you'll experience the will of God in your life as it is in heaven.

SERVE

There's a part of each of us that wants to be the greatest at something, if not everything. Wouldn't it be great to win every game, ace all the tests, and be noticed by all the right people? It is true that God desires us to do our best, but the path to significance begins with servant-hood. Jesus showed the full extent of his love when he took on a servant's role and washed his disciples' feet. This humbling experience is really quite empowering.

SERVE

The professor walked into the classroom and threw his well-worn leather satchel on the desk. It landed with a heavy thud, but not the thud of books. All the students turned to look as the teacher unsnapped the flap of the satchel. He removed an ancient brick and held it high over his head with one hand.

"This is a brick," he said. Then with his other hand, he pointed to a series of lithographs hanging behind him that captured the majesty of cathedrals and mansions. "These are constructed of bricks. A brick wants to belong to something greater than itself. The job of the architect is to figure out where the bricks belong. Let's get started."

Like bricks, believers belong to something greater than ourselves. We belong to the kingdom of God, and we have a purpose to fulfill: service. We discover our true sense of value and belonging when we serve.

GETTING STARTED

Look at the choices below and check the ones you feel reflect the greatness of God's perspective on service.

_____ to impress others	_____ do your own thing
_____ to impact others	_____ do what's right
_____ concern for gain	_____ instant gratification
_____ concern for giving	_____ lasting achievement
_____ praise of people	_____ to be served
_____ to honor God	_____ to serve others
_____ pleasure and fun	_____ controlling and competitive
_____ God's peace and joy	_____ self-control and cooperation

DISCOVERING THE TRUTH

Life isn't just a place to hang out and wait around until you get to heaven. Life is a training ground for greatness. In Psalm 71:17–21, God shows us that life is full of hardship at times. But those who work through and remain faithful, God will restore and fulfill in heaven. Greatness is a lofty goal for those walking as Jesus walked, but according to Matthew 23:11, greatness comes secondary to what?

_____

_____

_____

There's a path to greatness that is often overlooked. Read the following Scripture verses and list qualities or steps to becoming a servant.

1 Corinthians 4:2 _____

Matthew 18:1–4 _____

Matthew 20:28 _____

John 13:1–5 _____

Philippians 2:3–8 _____

EMBRACING THE TRUTH

[The only way you can serve God is by serving other people.
—Rick Warren]

Without looking to the Word, think about the life of Jesus Christ. From all the stories and knowledge you have about him, list all the ways Jesus was a great servant.

_____

_____

_____

_____

_____

Jesus gives great insight to the mystery of finding significance in serving. He tells us in his Word that when we serve others or "when you did it to one of the least of these" (Matthew 25:40 NLT), it's like we are doing it for Jesus. That brings tremendous blessing. However, what is true for the willing servant is true in reverse for the unwilling one. Jesus goes on to say in Matthew 25:45 (NLT), that when you don't serve, you are in essence "refusing to help me."

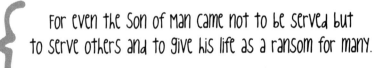

For even the Son of Man came not to be served but to serve others and to give his life as a ransom for many.
—Mark 10:45 NLT

Jesus doesn't ask anything from us that he wasn't willing to do himself. First Corinthians 4:1 indicates that one who follows Jesus should not only be a servant but should also be seen by others as a servant. So let's take an inventory on your life to see how others perceive you as a servant-hearted person.

Make a mark on the line indicating how others perceive you.

Others often wonder what makes me so much like Christ.

sometimes ———————————————— all the time

Others recognize servant leadership patterns in my lifestyle.

sometimes ———————————————— all the time

I put others ahead of myself.

sometimes ———————————————— all the time

I do something nice for others only if they've been nice to me.

sometimes ———————————————— all the time

I struggle with putting others first.

sometimes ———————————————— all the time

I don't mind if I don't get credit for something I did.

sometimes ———————————————— all the time

CONNECTING THE TRUTH

Take a look at the world you live in. There are needs in your school, church, and home. Think about the greatest needs around you. Now spend some time praying about those needs. List three great needs in your world right now.

1. _____

2. _____

3. _____

Servants meet needs. They look for ways to honor God and fulfill a need. How can you bring honor to God by meeting those needs listed above?

1. _____

2. _____

3. _____

According to Mark 9:41, greatness is not found in the size of the deed but in the humility of the servant. You may think you can't make a difference in this world or that you have nothing to offer. Remember this: being a servant starts with attitude. If you have a servant's attitude, you will do incredible things for the kingdom of God.

BRINGING IT HOME

Jesus taught that the way up is to go down. He taught his first disciples that the secret to becoming great is to become the servant of all. Looking beyond your own spiritual and physical needs and seeing others as Jesus sees them is a great measuring stick of your walk with Christ. You can find great significance when you serve others. Here are some ways to put your faith into action:

- **Volunteer** to teach a children's Sunday school class in your church.

- **Go** on a short-term missions trip.

- **Help** at a local homeless shelter or soup kitchen on a regular basis.

- **Pursue** opportunities to help those who are poor or in trouble.

- **Lead** a Bible study for people your own age.

OBEY

What is God requiring of you? Are you willing to give it? Is it to step outside your comfort zone so that somebody else can be comfortable? Is it to show love to somebody that, in your mind, doesn't deserve it? Jesus said, "But I will do what the Father requires of me, so that the world will know that I love the Father" (John 14:31). How much do you love the Father? How will others know of your love for him?

OBEY

> Indiana Jones: The ark of the covenant, the chest that the Hebrews used to carry around the ten commandments.
>
> Major Eaton: What, you mean the Ten Commandments?
>
> Indiana Jones: Yes, the actual ten commandments, the original stone tablets that Moses brought down from Mount Horeb and smashed, if you believe in that sort of thing. . . . Didn't any of you guys ever go to Sunday school?
>
> —*Indiana Jones: Raiders of the Lost Ark*

We all have rules to live by. You might as well face it; you will always have to answer to somebody. Mom and Dad, teachers and principals, professors and deans, bosses, and CEOs all stand in line ahead of us giving us instructions, expectations, and orders. Authority is a fact of life.

You may not have a choice in who has authority over you, but you can choose how to respond to that authority. When you respect authority, you are setting yourself up for God's blessing.

God created authority as a way to bring order to the chaos in this world.

The Bible has a lot to say about authority and how important it is for us to honor it. Jesus said, "I have been given all authority in heaven and on earth" (Matthew 28:18 NLT). In your new walk with Christ, he is your ultimate authority. Having trouble obeying and listening to others? When you fall in line with Jesus, he will give you the right attitude if you ask him.

GETTING STARTED

List at least a half dozen areas in your life in which you struggle to obey as a Christian.

1. _____

2. _____

3. _____

4. _____

5. _____

6. _____

Why do you feel you continue to struggle with these things?

_____

_____

_____

_____

DISCOVERING THE TRUTH

Read Matthew 7:24–27.

What do you take away from this story Jesus told?

_____

_____

_____

_____

We learn from this story that it simply isn't enough to read God's Word. God expects you to put his words into action. He expects you to see him as the ultimate authority in your life and trust him as you walk daily with him. Good servants understand the importance of obeying their master even before they know the outcome. This is the level of trust we need when we're following Christ. The great thing about our master is he has proven himself trustworthy time and time again. Therefore, you can trust God for what you do not yet know.

EMBRACING THE TRUTH

Think about the following men and women found in the Bible. How did they show extreme obedience in the way they stayed true to their commitments?

Abraham (James 2:21–24) _____

Rahab (James 2:25) _____

Abel (Hebrews 11:4) _____

Noah (Hebrews 11:7) _____

Moses' parents (Hebrews 11:23) _____

Moses (Hebrews 11:24–25) _____

Each of these individuals was obedient in the face of great risk. They were committed to God's authority, and they trusted God even when it seemed it could cost them their very lives.

CONNECTING THE TRUTH

[
I'm not out there sweating for three hours every day just to find out what it feels like to sweat.
]

—Michael Jordan

Obedience is not meaningless. We don't obey "just because." True obedience comes from a heart of love and expresses our commitment. There's no way the individuals you read about would have put their lives on the line if they didn't have a deep love for their master. If you're struggling with obeying God's Word, then maybe you're struggling with loving God. Jesus tells us time and time again in John 14 that those who love him are those who obey his teachings.

"If you love me, you will obey what I command" (John 14:15).

"Whoever has my commands and obeys them, he is the one who loves me. He who loves me will be loved by my Father, and I too will love him and show myself to him" (John 14:21).

"He who does not love me will not obey my teaching. These words you hear are not my own; they belong to the Father who sent me" (John 14:24).

What does Jesus say is the evidence of your love?

_____

_____

According to John 14:21, to whom does Jesus make himself known?

_____

_____

When you do what it takes to fall in love with Jesus, you will have no problem obeying him. He will make himself known to you. Submitting to God's authority is a result of a deep love you have for him. List the things you need to do to fall in love with God.

1. _____

2. _____

3. _____

4. _____

5. _____

6. _____

BRINGING IT HOME

Read Luke 6:46 out loud.

Read it out loud again.

Jesus asks the question in that verse to those who claim to know him but don't obey his word. Obeying authority comes down to trust and love. You can trust God because he wants the very best for you. You can love him because he first loved you. He sent his Son to die for your sins so that you would have eternal life with him. If you truly want to submit to his authority, then pray the following prayer.

Dear God,

I'm telling you now that I will strive to do all you instruct me to do, to the best of my ability, because I love you and I trust you.

Now go tell someone.

THRIVE

Doing God's will is the only "food" that really satisfies our souls. We spend much of our time finding different ways to be content, but Jesus promises that living God's will is the fullest and best life possible. Like Jesus, not everyone will understand or agree to this. They will challenge you and try to distract you. In the end, being obedient to God is worth it.

THRIVE

We have an invitation on our life. The call Jesus extended to the first disciples he also extends to you. It's the call of "Follow me" that rocks your world, changes your destination, brings peace, frustration, excitement, fulfillment, and fear . . . sometimes all at the same time. This invitation of Jesus, however, comes with stipulations. There's a price to pay. It will cost you something. First and foremost, you can't halfheartedly accept the invitation. It's all or nothing. To be half-committed is to be half-happy and halfway there. As the sovereign (supreme ruler) owner of all things, God expects us to demonstrate stewardship in every detail of life.

GETTING STARTED

When you hear the word *Christian*, what do you think? How does a Christian look to you? Make a list of how you think a totally dedicated, mature Christian behaves. Include what he or she does and what he or she avoids. In general, summarize the perfect Christian. Don't rush; spend some time on this.

The Perfect Christian

_____

_____

_____

_____

_____

Now think about your life. How do you measure up to the person you just described? Make a specific list of the obstacles that keep you from being consecrated (committed and dedicated) to God. In your list include any bad habits or distractions—anything and everything that prohibits you from being the "model Christian."

1. _____

2. _____

3. _____

4. _____

5. _____

DISCOVERING THE TRUTH

["For I know the plans I have for you," declares the Lord, "plans to prosper you and not to harm you, plans to give you hope and a future."]

—Jeremiah 29:11

{ We can't plan life. All we can do is be available for it. }

—Lauryn Hill

Here's a great question to ask yourself: What kind of life do I want to have? Jesus told us in John 10 that he came so we would have life to the fullest. Are you living life to the fullest? Check out the following scriptures as you think about your life and your plans.

"You were bought at a price. Therefore honor God with your body" (1 Corinthians 6:20).

"For who makes you different from anyone else? What do you have that you did not receive? And if you did receive it, why do you boast as though you did not?" (1 Corinthians 4:7).

"So then, each of us will give an account of himself to God" (Romans 14:12).

"Trust in the LORD with all your heart and lean not on your own understanding; in all your ways acknowledge him, and he will make your paths straight" (Proverbs 3:5–6).

EMBRACING THE TRUTH

[I don't want to survive! I want to live!]

—The captain from *WALL-E*

Every so often you need to stop and take an inventory of your life to examine your goals and determine if you're really living life to the fullest.

Take a few minutes right now and write out some of your goals: What do you want to do? Who do you want to be? What are some things you would like to accomplish? These can be short term (pass a test, get a good grade in a class) or long term (get accepted to college, have a certain career). Once you have your list, use the following questions to gauge the effect Christ has on your life in determining the choices you make.

- Have I honestly and objectively taken my life's goals before the Lord for his approval and guidance?

    _____ yes   _____ no

- Do my goals feed my own desire and ego more than they honor God?

    _____ yes   _____ no

- Am I willing to have Christ redirect my life, changing any goals I've set?

    _____ yes   _____ no

We all want to have purpose in life. We all want to live life to the fullest. The good news is that God wants that for us too. He wants the very best for us. In fact, his Word tells us that his will for our lives is good, pleasing, and perfect. Where is the pursuit of life's best taking you? Read Matthew 11:29–30. What does Jesus mean by "yoke"? What's the implication?

_____

_____

_____

_____

_____

CONNECTING THE TRUTH

{ It is not length of life, but depth of life. }
—Ralph Waldo Emerson

Look back to the list you made of the bad habits that keep you from being consecrated to God. What are some things you can do to overcome those areas of your life that rob you of God's greatest fulfillment for your life?

_____

_____

_____

_____

_____

Beware the danger so many of us encounter in believing discipleship is something we do. Surrendering to the Lord is not the same as being as obsessed with doing the things that are popular. Going to the right concerts, attending church, showing up at youth group, serving on mission trips, and having the right language are not the same as allowing God to shape your desires and dreams. True discipleship or following after God is making his obsessions your obsessions. It's when you submit to the authorities he appoints in your life, and you give him permission to do whatever he wants to do with you. This may or may not come easily, but it starts with a simple prayer of giving yourself to God, trusting that he has the best in store for you and your future. Take time right now to give yourself to God and his plans for your life.

BRINGING IT HOME

"If we live, we live to the Lord; and if we die, we die to the Lord. So, whether we live or die, we belong to the Lord" (Romans 14:8).

How are a willingness to live for God and a willingness to die for God related, and how does that willingness alter your life?

_____

_____

_____

_____

_____

If you're willing to die for God, then you must be willing to live for God. Embracing God's best for your life is about trusting God with the details of your life. What areas of your life do you need to trust God with? List them as prayer requests. Put them somewhere where you can see them as a reminder to surrender them to God.

WORSHIP

Your body is all you have to offer—you live in your body. The body enfolds your head (your mind and thoughts), your heart (your emotions and desires), your hands (your actions and plans), and your habits (your daily routine). The body represents the total person; it is the instrument by which all our service is given to God. In order to live for God, we must offer or give him all that we are, represented by our body. If our body is at God's disposal, he will have our free time, our pleasures, and all our behavior.

WORSHIP

You were made to worship. You can't help but worship. All that remains is to see who or what you will worship. But in order to have a true perspective on worship, you must first have a definition of what worship really is. Worship is not just singing. It doesn't just happen when the band strikes up or once or twice a week during service. It's all about attitude. Worship requires an attitude of humility—understanding that there's something bigger and better than you. True worship is a lifestyle that acknowledges and gives honor to God in all things.

{ Therefore, I urge you, brothers, in view of God's mercy, to offer your bodies as living sacrifices, holy and pleasing to God—this is your spiritual act of worship. }

—Romans 12:1

GETTING STARTED

It is only when men begin to worship that they begin to grow.

—Calvin Coolidge

Complete the following phrase fifteen times.

God is:

1. _____

2. _____

3. _____

4. _____

5. _____

6. _____

7. _____

8. _____

9. _____

10. _____

11. _____

12. _____

13. _____

14. _____

15. _____

DISCOVERING THE TRUTH

Lucius: You tell me where my suit is, woman! We are talking about the greater good!

Honey: "Greater good"? I am your wife! I'm the greatest good you are ever gonna get!

—*The Incredibles*

In actuality, God is the "greatest good" you will ever get. Realizing that is crucial in worshiping him. So why worship God? What is it about God that drives individuals to commit to him and worship him with all they are and do? What about you? What would it take to move you into worshiping God beyond the music and lip service and into a lifestyle that would seek to please him in all you do? Look up the following passages of Scripture and answer the question that still remains:

Why worship God?

James 2:21–24 _____

_____

_____

1 Chronicles 16:9 _____

_____

_____

Isaiah 40:12–14 _____

_____

_____

Psalm 147:11 _____

_____

_____

Mark 12:28–30 _____

_____

_____

EMBRACING THE TRUTH

To worship is to walk in humility with God. It's to acknowledge the great gap between Creator and creature. Worship begins with understanding who God is and where we place him in our lives.

Read Matthew 16:13–16.

When Jesus asked Peter, "Who do you say I am?" Peter replied, "You are the Christ, the Son of the living God." Peter knew who Jesus was. He knew Jesus was more than a good teacher. He knew Jesus was more than a man who was able to heal and perform miracles. Peter knew Jesus was indeed the Son of God. When it comes to worship, the first step is knowing who Jesus is.

Just as Jesus asked Peter, he asks you, "Who do you say I am?"
Take a minute to answer that question.

_____

_____

_____

_____

_____

CONNECTING THE TRUTH

{ God is Spirit, and his worshipers must worship in spirit and in truth. }

—John 4:24

So what does it mean to worship in spirit and truth?

_____

_____

_____

_____

_____

> Let the Word of Christ dwell in you richly as you teach and admonish one another with all wisdom, and as you sing psalms, hymns and spiritual songs with gratitude in your hearts to God.
>
> —Colossians 3:16

Worship is special. It opens a door that allows us to know God personally. It's not a religious activity that we turn on and off. It's not something we use to get something we want or to receive blessings. It's simply bringing honor and glory to God because of his greatness and love for us. There's a sense of awe and awareness (by faith) of having been with God. Walk through the following process to conduct a brief time of worship:

- Agree with God about who he is.

- Do a check on your life. Is there anything there that is not pleasing to God?

- If so, confess and receive God's forgiveness.

- Express your love for God.

- Ask God to help you be more like him.

- Surrender your will to God. Seek his way for your life.

- Trust God and walk in his promises.

BRINGING IT HOME

 The highest form of worship is the worship of unselfish Christian service. The greatest form of praise is the sound of consecrated feet seeking out the lost and helpless.

—Billy Graham

Peter's life was never the same after he met Jesus and began to worship him with his life. Peter left his job and his family to follow Jesus. Each day Peter had the opportunity to experience Jesus in action and to see that he was truly Lord. What are you doing on a daily basis to experience Jesus? What are you doing to really get to know him? It's when we truly know Jesus that we understand he is Lord and is worthy of our worship.

Picture Peter falling at the feet of Jesus and acknowledging him as Lord. Are you daily responding to Jesus in the same way? In your heart, are you doing what Jesus is asking of you? That is true worship.

GROW

When I was a kid people were forever comparing me with my older siblings. Maybe that happens to you, as well. Has anyone ever likened you to Jesus? The Scriptures tell us that we shall be like him. Just as we resemble our parents—whether in appearance or the way we speak or how we respond—we should also resemble Jesus in our actions and attitudes. It is part of our likeness to Christ. Who are you growing up to be like?

GROW

Everybody has dreams—ideas about what we want to become, accomplish, or be remembered for. It started when we would dream as kids of being race car drivers, superheroes, princesses, or movie stars. As the years go by, the dreams often remain, perhaps a bit more refined or more realistic. All too often, however, we fail to take the important step of action. Acting, stepping out and growing, is sometimes all that separates us from realizing our dreams.

There's a basic rule of science: Every living organism grows. If you're alive, you grow. More importantly, if you're alive in Christ, then you must grow.

GETTING STARTED

Take a look at the list below. Do your best (without looking at the answers) to match the celebrities with their jobs prior to achieving fame.

1. Jerry Seinfeld _____   A. member of the Royal Navy

2. Jon Bon Jovi _____   B. dug swimming pools

3. Mick Jagger _____   C. crafted holiday ornaments

4. Madonna _____   D. wore a chicken suit

5. Michael Dell _____   E. dishwasher

6. Brad Pitt _____   F. lightbulb retailer

7. David Letterman _____   G. hospital porter

8. Clint Eastwood _____   H. Dunkin' Donuts worker

9. Sean Connery _____   I. bricklayer

10. Whoopi Goldberg _____   J. weatherman

There's always room for growth. These celebrities all started out in one field or profession; but they weren't content to settle. They strived to become what they had always dreamed of becoming. Before Peter met Jesus, he was Simon the fisherman. After his encounter, he grew into Peter, a man of God who would help establish the church as we know it today. In our pursuit of God we have to be ready to grow. And growth brings change.

Answers: 1-F, 2-C, 3-G, 4-H, 5-E, 6-D, 7-J, 8-B, 9-A, 10-I

DISCOVERING THE TRUTH

Read the following Scripture verses and write out a growth principle that can be applied to your life. The first one is done for you.

Scripture	Growth Principle
Psalm 90:12	to gain wisdom
Psalm 92:12	_____
Isaiah 40: 31	_____
Luke 6:44	_____
2 Corinthians 10:15	_____
Ephesians 4:16	_____
Philippians 1:25	_____
Colossians 2:19	_____

EMBRACING THE TRUTH

"Lord, if it's You," Peter replied, "tell me to come
to You on the water."
"Come," he said.
Then Peter got down out of the boat, walked on the water
and came toward Jesus. But when he saw the wind, he was
afraid and, beginning to sink, cried out, "Lord, save me!"
Immediately Jesus reached out his hand and caught him.
"You of little faith," he said, "Why did you doubt?"

—Matthew 14:28–31

What an incredible moment of growth for Peter. Peter knew who Jesus was, had already seen some miracles, and had heard his message. However, now it was time to put his faith into action. Now it was time to grow up. Growing up can be difficult. We have to let go and trust even when we're not sure of the results.

So many times we begin to put our faith into action and take that first step of growth only to find ourselves sinking because we take our eyes off Jesus. The fears and doubts of the world can become overwhelming. Not growing becomes a stumbling block that prevents us from experiencing the power of faith. When was the last time you found yourself in Peter's sandals? Below are some areas that could be listed on a "growth chart of faith." Take a look and see how you're measuring up.

Sharing your faith

Healthy dating relationships

Things you watch

Things you listen to

Choices you make

Growth can be scary at times, but God wants to do incredible things in your life. It's when we take our eyes off of him that we experience "growing pains." That's what happened to Peter. Right in the middle of this moment of growth, Peter took his eyes off Jesus. He began to look at the world around him, and that's when fear and doubt washed over him. He began to sink. Fear and doubt immobilize growth. As you grow in Jesus, remember these two growth principles:

1. Look to Jesus.

Brothers, I do not consider myself yet to have taken hold of it. But one thing I do: Forgetting what is behind and straining toward what is ahead, I press on toward the goal to win the prize for which God has called me heavenward in Christ Jesus (Philippians 3:13–14).

2. Trust in Jesus.

Therefore I tell you, do not worry about your life, what you will eat or drink; or about your body, what you will wear. Is not life more important than food, and the body more important than clothes? Look at the birds of the air; they do not sow or reap or store away in barns, and yet your heavenly Father feeds them. Are you not much more valuable than they? Who of you by worrying can add a single hour to his life? (Matthew 6:25–27).

CONNECTING THE TRUTH

To be like Christ. That is our goal, plain and simple. It sounds peaceful, relaxing, easy, objective. But stop and think. He learned obedience by the things he suffered. So must we. It is neither easy nor quick nor natural. It is impossible in the flesh, slow in coming, and supernatural in scope. Only Christ can accomplish it within us.

—Chuck Swindoll

Read Psalm 27.

What happens when we stand up, look to Jesus, and overcome fear and doubt?

_____

_____

_____

_____

_____

_____

We don't have to be controlled by fear and doubt. What ways is Jesus asking you to grow in your faith?

_____

_____

_____

_____

_____

_____

BRINGING IT HOME

Answer the following questions the best you can:

What kind of person do you want to become?

_____

_____

_____

How do you want to be remembered?

_____

_____

_____

What great event would you like to be a part of?

_____

_____

_____

What's keeping you from taking the necessary actions to see these plans come to life?

_____

_____

_____

What fear or doubt is keeping you from growing in your faith?

_____

_____

_____

What does God want you to do in response?

_____

_____

_____

SET APART

Has anyone ever taken the blame for you? The truth is that we often get what we deserve. However, Jesus took the blame for our sin, and he now pleads to God on our behalf. We can become *set apart* because the one who called us is *set apart*. It's amazing when you think about it. When we are up against the wall and are weak in our commitments, our strength comes from one who remained perfect and sinless. Jesus is the only one qualified to redeem us. He has the highest place of honor, yet looks out for us . . . amazing!

SET APART

A young man had gone away to seminary. After three years of studying the Bible, Hebrew, Greek, and theology, he came home. Upon his arrival, friends and family greeted him with congratulations and celebration. During a reception in his honor, a question was raised: "What did you learn in all your years of education?"

After much thought the young man replied, "I learned a whole new vocabulary to explain what I did not understand."

To become set apart is to be holy. Now don't get scared into thinking this is too deep to understand! The good news is that to be set apart is not something you do; it's who you become. God tells us in his Word that he sets us apart. Look at his words to the nation of Israel, which still ring true for his people today: "You must be holy because I, the LORD, am holy. I have set you apart

from all other people to be my very own" (Leviticus 20:26 NLT).
As you grow closer to God, he will begin to set you apart for his
purpose to become his own. So when it comes to holiness, let
God do the work. Your part is to simply do the things that move
you closer to God.

GETTING STARTED

Rate each item based on the following holiness scale.			
1 = holy 2 = holiness depends on how it's used 3 = unholy			
The weekend football game	1	2	3
Movies at the theater	1	2	3
School dances	1	2	3
Fighting with brother or sister	1	2	3
Talking behind people's backs	1	2	3
Praying	1	2	3
Kissing at the back of the bus	1	2	3
Christians	1	2	3
Going to church	1	2	3
Making fun of others	1	2	3

Bad attitudes	1	2	3
Serving others	1	2	3
Sharing your faith	1	2	3
Watching TV	1	2	3
The music on your iPod	1	2	3
Trusting God	1	2	3

Look at the list and the answers you gave. Answer these three questions:

1. Are some things or activities holier than others?

_____

_____

_____

2. What determines holiness?

_____

_____

_____

3. How do you determine holiness?

_____

_____

_____

DISCOVERING THE TRUTH

[*It is God's will that you should be sanctified.*]

—1 Thessalonians 4:3

Sanctification is one of those words that you may have heard about but not really understood. However, it's important that you find understanding, because this is God's desire for you (1 Thessalonians 4:3). Since it's important to God, it needs to be important to you as well. So first things first; take a look at what Scripture says about the holiness of God.

"Save us, O LORD our God, and gather us from the nations, that we may give thanks to your holy name and glory in your praise" (Psalm 106:47).

"He provided redemption for his people; he ordained his covenant forever—holy and awesome is his name" (Psalm 111:9).

"The fear of the LORD is the beginning of wisdom, and knowledge of the Holy One is understanding" (Proverbs 9:10).

"Come and listen to my counsel. I'll share my heart with you and make you wise" (Proverbs 1:23 NLT).

"But the LORD Almighty will be exalted by his justice, and the holy God will show himself holy by his righteousness" (Isaiah 5:16).

"And they were calling to one another: 'Holy, holy, holy is the LORD Almighty; the whole earth is full of his glory'" (Isaiah 6:3).

"And I will put my Spirit in you and move you to follow my decrees and be careful to keep my laws" (Ezekiel 36:27).

"For the Mighty One has done great things for me—holy is his name" (Luke 1:49).

"We have not received the spirit of the world but the Spirit who is from God, that we may understand what God has freely given us" (1 Corinthians 2:12).

EMBRACING THE TRUTH

Jesus Christ came to make us holy, not to tell us to be holy; He came to do for us what we could not do for ourselves.

—Oswald Chambers

Do you know people who never forget anything? They're always prepared. It makes no difference what the situation, or what's needed, they've thought of everything. These people, although frustrating at times, provide a sense of security. We know they've covered all the bases.

God is like this. He's provided for you and me exactly what we need in our pursuit of becoming more and more like him. Becoming set apart is God working in us. Our part is to grow closer to him. This truth is vital to our understanding of what it means to become holy.

Look at the following Scripture verses to see what God's part is in your becoming holy.

Amos 4:2	His character is holy.
1 Peter 1:14–16	He calls us to be holy.
1 Corinthians 6:11	He creates holiness in us.

Now look up the following Scripture verses and list your part concerning holiness:

Hebrews 12:10 _____

Romans 12: 1–2 _____

Ephesians 5:1–2 _____

CONNECTING THE TRUTH

Most people love Christmas morning. The anticipation of gifts from friends and family is very exciting. And that excitement is based on the promise of great gifts.

In our pursuit of being holy, God has sent us an incredible gift. He sent the Holy Spirit to be a gift to everyone who trusts in Jesus Christ as Savior. John 16:7 tells us, "But I tell you the truth: It is for your good that I am going away. Unless I go, the Counselor will not come to you; but if I go, I will send him to you."

Read John 16:5–16 and answer the following questions:

Where was Jesus going?

_____

_____

_____

Who or what exactly is this Counselor?

_____

_____

_____

Why did Jesus have to leave someone behind?

_____

_____

_____

What benefit is the Spirit to you?

_____

_____

_____

What will the Holy Spirit do?

_____

_____

_____

How do you know he'll give you good advice?

_____

_____

_____

What kind of guidelines does this Counselor give?

_____

_____

_____

BRINGING IT HOME

God cares about your everyday life. His desire for you is to be holy because he is holy. This is so important to God that he has provided the Holy Spirit to direct you in how to live. Are there areas in your life in which you have not allowed the Holy Spirit to give you counsel? Take time now to release those areas as you trust God and grow in your relationship with him.

Take a look back over the last several weeks. Before God, ask yourself these questions:

1. Am I where I thought I would be spiritually? Personally?

_____

_____

_____

2. Am I moving and growing in my relationship with Jesus?

_____

_____

_____

3. What steps do I need to take to keep growing?

_____

_____

_____

"Whoever claims to live in him must walk as Jesus did" (1 John 2:6).

AFTERWORD

A rabbi was walking on an ancient trail one day all by himself. His disciples had gone ahead of him, and he took advantage of the quiet time to recite some Scripture.

Soon he came to a fork in the trail. The rabbi was so focused on the passage of Scripture and what God was saying to him that he went right instead of left. Left would have taken him to the place where his disciples were waiting for him. Right took him outside of town to a small Roman fort built to protect the road nearby. The rabbi was not even aware of where he was until he found himself in front of the gate where the Roman soldier stood guard. The centurion on the wall shouted at him, "Who are you? What are you doing here?"

The somewhat startled rabbi said, "What?"

"Who are you? What are you doing here?"

This time the rabbi's voice came back with confidence. "What do you get paid to ask those questions?"

The soldier replied, "Two denarii a week. Why?"

"I'll give you double if you stand outside my house and ask me those two questions every morning when I leave home."

Who am I and what am I doing here? Those questions set us on a journey. The problem is that most young people, and perhaps quite a few adults, don't know who they are and what they are here for. Pursuing the answers to those questions shapes and forms our lives. C. S. Lewis said it's not *if* you're being formed, it's *who* or *what* is forming you. We're constantly being formed and conformed to one image or another or in one philosophy or another.

Who you are and what you're doing here is not answered in a statement but defined in a journey. *iFollow* has put you on a journey that will begin to shape your life. As you grow closer to God, you will find fulfillment and his purpose for your life. And that is what it means to be a disciple.

So think clearly and exercise self-control. Look forward to the gracious salvation that will come to you when Jesus Christ is revealed to the world. So you must live as God's obedient children. Don't slip back into your old ways of living to satisfy your own desires. You didn't know any better then. But now you must be holy in everything you do, just as God who chose you is holy (1 Peter 1:13–15 NLT).